What's the Difference Between a

BUTTERFLY
and a
MOTH?

by Robin Koontz-Dacey

Illustrated by Bandelin-Dacey

Picture Window Books
Minneapolis, Minnesota

Look up! What is that beautiful winged creature
dancing high in the sky? Is it a butterfly,
or is it a moth?

Thanks to our advisers for their expertise, research, and advice:

Celeste Welty, Ph.D.
Extension Entomologist & Associate Professor of Entomology
Ohio State University

Terry Flaherty, Ph.D., Professor of English
Minnesota State University, Mankato

Editor: Shelly Lyons
Designer: Abbey Fitzgerald
Page Production: Melissa Kes
Art Director: Nathan Gassman
Editorial Director: Nick Healy
Creative Director: Joe Ewest
The illustrations in this book were created with watercolor.

Photo credit: Shutterstock/siloto (handmade paper), 1 and 22 (background)
and throughout in sidebars and titlebars.

Picture Window Books
151 Good Counsel Drive
P.O. Box 669
Mankato, MN 56002-0669
877-845-8392
www.picturewindowbooks.com

Library of Congress Cataloging-in-Publication Data
Koontz, Robin Michal.
What's the difference between a butterfly and a moth? /
by Robin Koontz ; illustrated by Bandelin-Dacey.
p. cm. —(What's the difference?)
Includes index.
ISBN 978-1-4048-5543-4 (library binding)
1. Butterflies—Juvenile literature. 2. Moths—Juvenile literature.
I. Bandelin, Debra, ill. II. Dacey, Bob, ill. III. Title.
QL544.2.K66 2010
595.78—dc22
                                                              2009006884

Butterflies and moths can look a lot alike. Can you spot the differences between the two?

All butterflies and moths begin life as caterpillars. Caterpillars like to munch on leaves and flowers.

Caterpillars start to swell from all the food they eat. When their skin gets too tight, they molt, or shed their skin. New skin lets them keep eating and growing.

The period of time between each molting is called an instar.

A butterfly and a moth start out the same, but each of them changes in different ways. A butterfly caterpillar fixes one of its ends to a leaf or other object. Then it is time to change into a butterfly.

Its tight skin bursts open to show new skin. The new skin hardens and becomes a protective shell. The shell is called a chrysalis.

chrysalis

1

2

3

The chrysalis can look like a twig, dead leaf, or drop of water. It is like a safe house for the caterpillar. Inside the chrysalis, the caterpillar slowly changes into its adult form.

When it is time to change into an adult, a moth caterpillar usually fixes itself to a plant, leaf, or piece of bark. Some moth caterpillars dig themselves into the ground to hide. Most of them then spin a cocoon, which is a silky casing.

1

2

cocoon

3

Metamorphosis is the process of a caterpillar becoming a butterfly or moth. *Metamorphosis* means "change in form."

Butterflies and moths have a proboscis. They use this organ like a straw to suck up nectar from flowers.

Butterflies, moths, other insects, and even some bats spread a yellow powder called pollen from flower to flower. Pollination, or spreading pollen, helps fruits and vegetables grow.

Can you spot the proboscis? Look closely as a butterfly or a moth sips and zips from flower to flower. When the animal isn't using the proboscis, the organ is curled up.

proboscis

Is it a butterfly or a moth doing all that sipping? Most butterflies are diurnal. That means they flutter around only during daytime hours.

Most moths are nocturnal. They fly around only at night.
That's when the birds that like to eat moths are sleeping.

Can you spot the difference between a butterfly and a moth by looking at the wings? Many butterflies have wings that are covered with thousands of bright, colorful scales. The colors help the insect blend in with its surroundings. Spots on its wings can look like large eyes that scare away animals.

Most moths have wings that are covered with dull-colored scales to match their resting places. Some moths look like wood or a leaf. This helps them blend into their surroundings.

Some animals and insects are camouflaged. That means they are shaped or colored to match their surroundings. Camouflage helps them hide from enemies .

Something else about wings shows us the difference between a butterfly and a moth. Watch the insect land and come to rest. Are the wings pointed to the sky or held flat over the insect's body? Most of the time, a butterfly's wings are pointed upward.

A moth's wings usually are held flat over its body when the insect is at rest.

Body shape is another difference between butterflies and moths. Most butterflies have thin bodies. Because butterflies flutter around during warm sunny days, they do not need extra fat.

Most moths have plump bodies. Many moth bodies are furry. Moths need the extra fat and fur to keep them cozy as they flit through the cool night air.

Like all insects, butterflies and moths have bodies made up of a head, thorax, and abdomen.

There is another way to tell the difference between a butterfly and a moth. If you look closely, you will see that a butterfly has two thin feelers. The feelers have thick ends. Sometimes the feelers look like tiny clubs.

A moth has two feelers that can be thin or thick. Sometimes the feelers look like fuzzy feathers.

Now you know lots of differences between a butterfly and a moth!

Feelers are called antennae.

BUTTERFLY

caterpillar
makes a
cocoon

thin body

abdomen

thorax

proboscis

head

wings point
upward

bright colors
blend in with
surroundings

thin, club-like
antennae

caterpillar makes
a chrysalis

proboscis

head

thick antennae

proboscis

thorax

abdomen

thick, furry
body

wings held flat
over the body

MOTH

dull colors
blend in with
surroundings

Fun Facts

Butterflies and moths are the only members of the group of insects called Lepidoptera. *Lepidoptera* is the Greek word for "scale wing."

People have found about 20,000 kinds of butterflies and 150,000 kinds of moths in the world. But there are probably many that are yet to be discovered.

The black scales on the wings of many butterflies help soak up heat from the sun.

The hummingbird hawkmoth flies during the day. It hovers in front of flowers, just like a hummingbird.

Every fall, monarch butterflies migrate thousands of miles to places in the far south, like Mexico. One tagged butterfly flew at least 1,870 miles (2,992 kilometers).

Glossary

abdomen—the part of an insect's body that is attached to the thorax and is not the head

antennae—feelers on an insect's head used to sense and touch smells; *antennae* is the word for more than one antenna

caterpillar—a young butterfly or moth that is in the stage of growth when it looks like a worm with legs

chrysalis—the shell in which a caterpillar changes into a butterfly

cocoon—a covering made by a caterpillar to protect itself as it changes into a moth

diurnal—awake or active during the day

insect—a small, six-legged animal; butterflies, moths, bees, and flies are examples of insects

instar—the period of time between molting

metamorphosis—changing from one form into a very different form, like a caterpillar to a butterfly

molt—to shed fur, feathers, or an outer layer of skin

nocturnal—awake or active at night

pollination—the process of carrying pollen from the male part of a flower to the female part

proboscis—a long, slender organ that looks like a straw

thorax—the middle part of an insect's body

To Learn More

More Books to Read

Bishop, Nic. *Nic Bishop Butterflies and Moths*. New York: Scholastic Nonfiction, 2009.

Collier-Morales, Roberta. *Butterflies and Moths*. New York: Grosset & Dunlap, 2001.

Slade, Suzanne. *From Caterpillar to Butterfly: Following the Life Cycle*. Minneapolis: Picture Window Books, 2009.

Internet Sites

FactHound offers a safe, fun way to find Internet sites related to this book. All of the sites on FactHound have been researched by our staff.

Here's all you do:

Visit *www.facthound.com*

FactHound will fetch the best sites for you!

Index

Look for all of the books in the What's the Difference? series:

What's the Difference Between a Butterfly and a Moth?

What's the Difference Between a Frog and a Toad?

What's the Difference Between a Leopard and a Cheetah?

What's the Difference Between an Alligator and a Crocodile?